Cooking with

PASTA

ESSENTIAL 101 TIPS

Cooking with

PASTA

CONTRIBUTING EDITOR
Anne Willan

DORLING KINDERSLEY
London • New York • Stuttgart

A DORLING KINDERSLEY BOOK

Editor Irene Lyford
Art Editor Louise Bruce
Managing Editor Mary-Clare Jerram
Managing Art Editor Amanda Lunn
Production Controller Meryl Silbert

First published in Great Britain in 1995 by
Dorling Kindersley Limited,
9 Henrietta Street, London WC2E 8PS

A CIP catalogue record for this book is available from the British Library

ISBN 07513-0183-3

Computer page make-up Mark Bracey
Text film output by The Right Type, Great Britain
Reproduced by Colourscan
Printed and bound by Graphicom, Italy

ESSENTIAL TIPS

_____ PAGES 8-13 _____

WHICH PASTA?

1 ....Calorie count
2 ....Choosing dried or fresh pasta
3 ....Buy fresh pasta
4 ....Dried pasta choice
5 ....Long pasta
6 ....Short pasta shapes
7 ....Stuffed & layered
8 ....Little pasta for soup
9 ....Oriental pasta
10 ....Match sauce to pasta

_____ PAGES 14-19 _____

STORE-CUPBOARD BASICS

11 ....Which flour?
12 ....Eggs
13 ....Olive oil
14 ....Herbs
15 ....Spices
16 ....Garlic & onions

17 ....Tomatoes
18 ....Olives & capers
19 ....Spinach
20 ....Pine nuts
21 ....Balsamic vinegar
22 ....Ham & bacon
23 ....Cheeses for pasta

_____ PAGES 20-23 _____

HOW TO MAKE FRESH PASTA

24 ....Fresh egg pasta dough
25 ....Machine-mix
26 ....Add flavours
27 ....Colour pasta dough
28 ....Traditional rolling pin
29 ....Roll pasta dough by hand
30 ....Machine-roll
31 ....Drying pasta

_____ PAGES 24-26 _____

How to Cut &
Stuff Pasta

32 .... Machine-cut
33 .... Useful cutters
34 .... Cutting ribbons by hand
35 .... Cut flat sheets
36 .... Pipe pasta fillings
37 .... Folded-stuffed pasta
38 .... Sandwich-stuffed pasta

_____ PAGES 27-31 _____

Cook & Serve
Pasta

39 .... Pasta portions
40 .... Saucepan size
41 .... Pasta-to-water
42 .... Fast-boil pasta
43 .... Add pasta to water
44 .... Pasta drainer
45 .... Is it ready?
46 .... Drain & rinse
47 .... Serve hot
48 .... Toss quickly
49 .... Pan-fry pasta
50 .... Deep-frying
51 .... Prevent sticking
52 .... Avoid a crust
53 .... Perfect partners
54 .... Garnishes
55 .... How to eat long pasta

_____ PAGES 32-40 _____

Pasta Soups
& Salads

56 .... Minestrone soup
57 .... Vegetable noodle soup
58 .... Fusilli & pesto salad
59 .... Hot parsley pasta salad
60 ...... Fresh tuna pasta salad Niçoise
61 .... Asian noodle salad

_____ PAGES 41-52 _____

Pasta Sauces

62 .... Classic béchamel sauce
63 .... Fresh tomato sauce
64 .... Pesto sauce
65 .... Freeze pesto portions
66 .... Carbonara
67 .... Serving carbonara sauce
68 .... Egg & anchovy
69 .... Gorgonzola
70 .... Seafood sauce
71 .... Tomato & basil sauce

72......Anchovy, olive, & caper sauce
73.................Spicy tomato & bacon
74...........................Primavera sauce
75............................Ragù Bolognese
76....................Butter & cream sauce
77.........................White clam sauce
78............................Red clam sauce
79...........Olive oil & garlic dressing
80...............................Three cheeses
81.........Choosing & cooking cheese

PAGES 53-67

STUFFED & BAKED PASTA

82.....................................Meat filling
83................................Cheese filling
84........Spinach & cheese pinwheels
85....................Cheese tortellini with
                              smoked salmon
86............Prevent tortellini bursting
87................Aubergine lasagne with
                                  cheese sauce
88........................Lasagne bolognese
89....................Macaroni with fennel
                                      & raisins
90...........Ravioli with saffron ricotta
91.............................Delicate pastas
92......Cannelloni with chicken &
                                   mozzarella
93.................Baked rigatoni with
                                    meatballs
94.............Chinese moons with
                                  lemon sauce

PAGES 68-69

STORE & REHEAT PASTA

95..............................Store dry pasta
96......................Fresh pasta storage
97..........Prepare & store pasta salad
98...............................Freeze sauces
99...................................Defrost well
100....................................Refrigerate
101...............................Reheat pasta

INDEX 70
ACKNOWLEDGMENTS 72

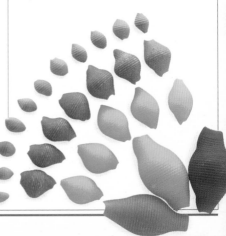

WHICH PASTA?

1 CALORIE COUNT

Pasta is an excellent source of carbohydrate, yet it is surprisingly low in calories. Protein and fibre content varies according to whether the pasta is made with or without eggs and which type of flour is used.

Typical analysis – cooked pasta 28g (1oz)	Kcal	Fibre
Plain spaghetti	38	0.3g
Wholewheat spaghetti	30	0.9g
Tagliatelle (egg pasta)	41	0.3g
Tagliatelle verde	37	0.3g

2 CHOOSING DRIED OR FRESH PASTA

Dried, commercially made pasta is an essential store-cupboard stand-by, providing the basis for a quick, cheap, and nutritious meal. Fresh, home-made egg pasta is deliciously light and inexpensive, but does take time to prepare. Shop-bought, fresh pasta, served with a simple home-made sauce, provides a fast, elegant, but more expensive, alternative.

3 BUY FRESH PASTA

Commercially made, fresh egg pasta is widely available in a variety of shapes, colours, and flavours as well as in ready-stuffed forms such as tortellini and ravioli. If possible, buy it from a specialist delicatessen or a reputable retailer; check information on packages and avoid any nearing their "sell-by" date.

STUFFED PASTA

4 DRIED PASTA CHOICE

Look for commercially produced dried pasta made from 100% pure durum wheat or semolina. Choose a wholewheat variety for higher fibre content, or "*verde*" for the spinach-flavoured version. Avoid packets with dusty crumbs in the bottom: this may suggest that the pasta is stale.

FARFALLE

5 LONG PASTA

There are two basic forms of long pasta: string shapes, such as spaghetti, and ribbons, such as tagliatelle. Commercially made string shapes are based on a simple flour and water paste, whereas ribbons often contain egg.

All are available fresh or dried and come in a range of sizes and in a variety of flavours, such as spinach, tomato, or wholewheat. Ribbons are the most popular home-made pasta, as they are the easiest shape to cut, either by hand or machine.

CAPPELLINI

PAPPARDELLE

TAGLIATELLE VERDE

TAGLIARINI

SPAGHETTI

BUCKWHEAT SPAGHETTI

WHOLEWHEAT SPAGHETTI

6 SHORT PASTA SHAPES

This group consists of a huge variety of shapes: tubes, shells, spirals, bows, rings, and wheels. Most of these shapes are commercially produced, dried pasta, made of flour and water paste, and are often available in different flavours or colours. Each shape has its own Italian name, which usually describes the object it resembles: for example, conchiglie (shell); farfalle (butterfly); lumache (snail); and ruoti (wheel).

TUBETTI LUNGHI

FARFALLE

CHIFFERI RIGATI

CAPPELLETTI

RIGATONI

RUOTI

MILLERIGHE

GIGANTONI

DITALINI

CONCHIGLIE

STROZZAPRETI

7 STUFFED & LAYERED

Small pasta shapes, such as tortelloni, are stuffed with savoury fillings, whereas in layered dishes, sheets of pasta (lasagne) are alternated with sauce and filling. For cannelloni, pasta rectangles are rolled up with a filling inside, topped with a sauce, and baked.

LASAGNE VERDE

CANNELLONI

LASAGNE

TORTELLONI VERDE

RAVIOLI

RIDGED LASAGNE VERDE

8 LITTLE PASTA FOR SOUP

Pastina – literally "little pasta" – is made in an immense variety of attractive and amusing shapes. Use pastina in light broths and simple children's dishes.

DITALINI

ORZO

ALPHABETTI

STELLINI

9 ORIENTAL PASTA

Many oriental noodles can be cooked in the same way as Italian pasta, but cellophane noodles and rice sticks are soaked before use. Crispy wontons, and some mung-bean-starch noodles, are deep-fried.

CHINESE NOODLES

FINE DRIED EGG NOODLES

DRIED EGG NOODLES

FRESH NOODLES

10 MATCH SAUCE TO PASTA

Each pasta shape is suited to a particular type of sauce: home-made ribbons absorb butter- and cream-based sauces particularly well, while string shapes are best with sauces that cling – for example those based on olive oil. Short pasta shapes are ideal with chunky sauces that get caught up in the folds and hollows, while small stuffed pastas require sauces that complement the filling without overwhelming it.

SPAGHETTI
Bolognese sauce clings well to long strands of spaghetti.

FUSILLI AL PESTO
Pesto, a classic basil sauce, suits long and short pasta.

SPINACH-CHEESE ROLLS
The red-pepper sauce adds a striking counterpoint.

STORE-CUPBOARD BASICS

11 WHICH FLOUR?

To make egg pasta, use either strong white flour or an unbleached plain flour. Semolina flour is not suitable for home-made pasta as it is hard to roll by hand. For extra fibre content, you can use equal amounts of wholemeal and white flour.

UNBLEACHED PLAIN FLOUR

12 EGGS

Use the freshest eggs possible for home-made pasta. Immerse in water to test freshness: a new-laid egg will float on its side. Store eggs in the refrigerator but, for pasta dough, bring to room temperature before use.

NEW-LAID EGG

13 OLIVE OIL

Olive oil is a natural partner for pasta dishes – whether served as a condiment, or used in marinades and sauces. Choose unrefined oil from the first, cold pressing of the olives. "Extra-virgin" describes the best European oil.

TOP-QUALITY OLIVE OIL

14 HERBS

Fresh herbs have the best flavour. If buying dried herbs, look for whole rather than chopped leaves. Use dried herbs sparingly: they have a stronger taste than fresh herbs.

PARSLEY
Parsley provides both flavour and garnish.

BASIL
The peppery flavour of basil is well suited to tomato-based dishes.

SAGE
Enhance pasta sauces with the subtle flavour of finely chopped fresh sage leaves.

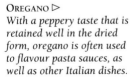

THYME
Use fresh or dried sprigs or dried leaves for pungent seasoning. If using sprigs, remove before serving.

OREGANO ▷
With a peppery taste that is retained well in the dried form, oregano is often used to flavour pasta sauces, as well as other Italian dishes.

◁ MARJORAM
Marjoram is related to oregano but has a more delicate aroma. This herb is best used fresh.

15 SPICES

Buy whole spices, store them in well-sealed containers, and grind only when required. Try to select spices that complement the main dish ingredients.

JUNIPER BERRIES
Use fresh or dried to flavour meat or vegetable dishes.

NUTMEG
A little freshly grated nutmeg contributes a distinctive flavour to milk-based sauces.

SALT
Add salt with caution, using your own taste to decide on the right amount.

BLACK PEPPER
Black pepper is more pungent than white.

SAFFRON
Saffron, available as strands or as a powder, provides colour and flavour.

16 GARLIC & ONIONS

Garlic and onions vary in flavour according to variety: red-skinned garlic and the common yellow onion are the strongest tasting. Fry garlic gently as it burns easily and becomes acrid.

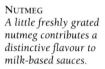

△ **GARLIC**
Buy fresh, firm heads of garlic.

▽ **ONION**
Choose firm, dry bulbs with no black or powdery spots.

17 TOMATOES

The tomato, either fresh or in one of its many preserved forms, is often a vital ingredient in pasta recipes. Outdoor-grown, sun-ripened tomatoes have the best flavour of all.

COMMON TOMATO
Serve raw in salads and as a garnish, or peel, seed, and chop for soups and sauces.

PLUM TOMATO
Plum tomatoes have few seeds and excellent flavour.

CHERRY TOMATOES
Serve these tiny, flavour-packed tomatoes whole for a colourful pasta garnish.

TOMATO PURÉE IN A TUBE
A tube of tomato purée is useful as it can be resealed after using a small amount.

SUN-DRIED TOMATOES
Available dried or stored in oil, a small quantity adds a distinctive flavour.

CHOPPED TINNED TOMATOES
Press through sieve with a spoon for passata sauce.

WHOLE TINNED TOMATOES
The best plum tomatoes are from San Marzano, Italy.

TINNED TOMATO PURÉE
For the best flavour, use double concentrated purée.

18 OLIVES & CAPERS

For a simple pasta sauce, mix puréed olives
with a little oil. Slightly more elaborate is a sauce that
combines anchovies, olives, and capers (*see p.45*).

GREEN
OLIVES

CAPERS
*Add capers
towards the
end of cooking
time as heat
intensifies
their flavour
and saltiness.*

VINEGAR-PACKED CAPERS

SALTED CAPERS

OLIVES
*Olives that are packed
in oil or vinegar can
be kept at room
temperature,
but refrigerate
canned olives
after opening.*

BLACK
OLIVES

19 SPINACH

Frozen, chopped spinach is a
useful store-cupboard stand-by; use
it to colour and flavour home-made
pasta dough for pasta verde, or mix
with ricotta cheese for a delicious
stuffing. Whether you use fresh or
frozen spinach, you must squeeze it
thoroughly to remove all excess
moisture after cooking and draining.

20 PINE NUTS

Toast pine
nuts to enhance
their sweet flavour.
Use them whole
or ground as in
pesto, the well-known
Italian basil-based sauce.

BLANCHED PINE NUTS

21 BALSAMIC VINEGAR

True balsamic
vinegar, which is aged
for several years, is
very expensive. For
use in sauces and
salads, look for a
cheaper, younger
version with a
rich flavour.

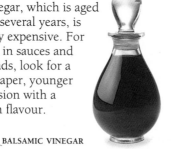

BALSAMIC VINEGAR

22 HAM & BACON

Many pasta recipes call for a
quantity of ham or bacon. This is
often diced or cut into thin strips
and sautéed, to add flavour and
texture to sauces. Parma is one of
several fine Italian hams.

Pancetta is another regional Italian
speciality – a type of bacon that is
cured like ham. If you cannot find
Pancetta, use good quality, lean,
smoked bacon instead.

23 CHEESES FOR PASTA

When buying hard cheeses such as Parmesan, ask for a piece to be cut from the whole cheese rather than choosing a pre-cut piece sealed in plastic. Wrap the cheese in foil and keep it in the refrigerator. Keep fresh and soft cheeses in the refrigerator in an airtight container.

◁ **MOZZARELLA**
This creamy, mild cheese melts well for a pasta topping. Keep refrigerated in brine, 2–3 days.

△ **PECORINO ROMANO**
A hard cheese made from sheep's milk, this is similar to Parmesan, but has a sharper flavour.

△ **RICOTTA**
Frequently used as the basis for pasta fillings, ricotta is a delicate, creamy fresh cheese.

△ **FONTINA**
A semi-hard cheese with a smoky taste, fontina melts easily in sauces.

△ **GORGONZOLA**
An Italian blue cheese with a sharp flavour.

△ **MASCARPONE**
A fresh, double-cream, soft dessert cheese.

PARMIGIANO △ **REGGIANO**
A hard, grainy cheese, this is the correct name for Parmesan cheese.

19

HOW TO MAKE FRESH PASTA

24 FRESH EGG PASTA DOUGH
Makes 500 g (1 lb)

Ingredients
300 g (10 oz) plain flour
3 eggs
15 ml (1 tbsp) oil

1 ▷ Mound sifted flour on surface; add eggs, oil, and pinch of salt.

2 ▷ With fingertips, combine eggs, oil, and salt. Gradually work in flour to form dough; add more flour if sticky.

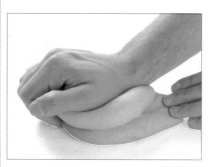

3 Scrape dough from work surface and form into ball; on floured surface, knead dough until elastic and smooth.

4 Form dough into ball and cover with bowl. Leave to rest for one hour at room temperature before rolling out.

25 MACHINE-MIX
Put flour, oil, and salt (*see p.20 for quantities*) into processor; add eggs one at a time, pulsing briefly between each. Process until dough is well mixed; form into ball.

ADD EGGS TO FLOUR

26 ADD FLAVOURS
For pasta verde, add 75 g (2½ oz) cooked, drained, squeezed dry, and chopped spinach per egg. For tomato-flavoured pasta, add 1 tablespoon purée per egg. Add flavourings to the flour with the eggs.

PASTA VERDE

ADD SPINACH WITH EGGS

27 COLOUR PASTA DOUGH
Add the ingredients suggested below to colour your pasta dough (they have little effect on taste). You may need to add more flour to absorb the extra moisture.

SAFFRON
For a warm, golden-coloured dough, add a large pinch of ground saffron with the eggs.

BEETROOT
Colour pasta dough pink with 1 tablespoon of puréed, cooked beetroot per egg.

BASIL
Finely chop 2 tbsp fresh basil leaves. Work into the flour with the eggs.

MUSHROOM
Lightly cook ½ lb mushrooms; drain well and purée; add to flour with eggs.

28 TRADITIONAL ROLLING PIN

Italian pasta cooks use a long, thin rolling pin with no handles. The extra length is useful as the dough covers a large area when rolled out.

ROLLING BY HAND
This traditional pasta pin is 80 cm (32 in) long.

29 ROLL PASTA DOUGH BY HAND

Remove dough from under upturned bowl. Before beginning to roll, knead dough briefly on floured surface to work back any moisture that has appeared on surface. Form dough into ball with hands.

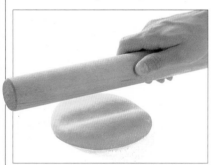

1 Sprinkle surface with flour. Place ball of dough on work surface and flatten it slightly with rolling pin. Begin rolling out dough, turning and moving it all the time to prevent it sticking.

2 Continue rolling, pressing dough away from you, not pushing down, and always rolling in just one direction. Sprinkle work surface and rolling pin generously with flour as you work.

3 Keeping even pressure on rolling pin, carry on rolling until dough is almost transparent. If rolling pin is not long enough, divide dough into three and roll each piece separately. Keep other pieces wrapped in clingfilm.

30 MACHINE-ROLL

A pasta machine gradually kneads the dough as it is rolled; it is not necessary to knead by hand.

1 Divide dough into three or four pieces and dust lightly with flour. Set machine rollers to widest setting and feed through one piece of dough.

2 Fold strip into thirds or quarters to form square; feed through machine again. Repeat folding and rolling seven to ten times until dough is smooth.

3 Tighten rollers one notch and feed dough through again. Continue rolling, tightening rollers one notch at a time, and ending with narrowest setting. Dust with flour if dough becomes sticky. Repeat with remaining pieces.

31 DRYING PASTA

When the pasta dough has been rolled out as thinly as possible, hang the pieces over a broom handle suspended between two chairs, or over the edge of a work surface. Leave the pasta to dry until it acquires a leathery look, 5–10 minutes, before cutting into the desired shapes.

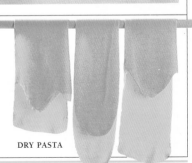

DRY PASTA

How to Cut & Stuff Pasta

32 Machine-Cut

Only machine-rolled pasta can be cut by machine. Attach the cutters and select the required width setting. Pass each strip of dough through the machine.

Dry Pasta
Let pasta dry for 1–2 hours before cooking or storing.

33 Useful Cutters

A pastry wheel is perfect for cutting and sealing stuffed pasta and for cutting ribbons, whereas biscuit cutters are ideal for cutting out pasta circles for stuffing. A sharp chef's knife is also useful.

BISCUIT CUTTERS

PASTRY WHEEL

CHEF'S KNIFE

34 Cutting Ribbons by Hand

Sprinkle the rolled-out dough with flour, then roll it up loosely. With a sharp knife, cut across into ribbons of the required width: fettuccine, for example, is about 5 mm (¼ in) wide.

Carefully unravel the ribbons and sprinkle with flour. Lay them flat, or loosely coiled on a floured tea towel, and leave to dry for 1–2 hours.

CUT RIBBONS TO DESIRED WIDTH

35 CUT FLAT SHEETS

When the rolled-out dough has dried a little, cut it with a long, sharp knife. For cannelloni, cut into 7.5 x 15 cm (3 x 6 in) rectangles. For lasagne, cut into pieces 5 cm (2 in) wide and long enough to fit your baking dish. Sprinkle with flour and leave to dry for 1–2 hours.

CUT DOUGH ON FLOURED BOARD

36 PIPE PASTA FILLINGS

Spoon filling into a piping bag and push down to exclude any air. Twist end and hold tightly in one hand then, with the other hand, squeeze gently at the top of the bag to start the filling flowing.

GENTLY SQUEEZE BAG

37 FOLDED-STUFFED PASTA

For folded-stuffed pasta, roll the dough out as thinly as possible. Place the stuffing in the centre of each disc or square, fold over, and pinch the edges to seal. Leave to dry for 1–2 hours.

1 For tortellini, cut 5 cm (2 in) discs from pasta dough. Place some filling in centre of each disc.

2 Wet edge of disc; fold in half and seal edges. Curve around finger then pinch ends together.

PANSOTI AND CAPPELLETTI
Both are folded and stuffed squares; cappelletti are then curved into a hat shape.

38 Sandwich-Stuffed Pasta

In this form of stuffed pasta, the filling is sandwiched between two layers of dough, which are then cut into squares or circles. Roll the pasta as thinly as possible – not more than 1.5 mm (¹⁄₁₆ in) thick.

SMALL RAVIOLI

LARGE RAVIOLI

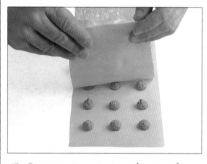

1 Cut pasta into two equal rectangles. Moisten surface of one sheet with water. Pipe small mounds of filling on the dough, spaced 4 cm (1½ in) apart.

2 Lay second rectangle on top. Press floured piping tube over mounds to seal dough around filling. Press around mounds with fingers to seal layers.

3 With fluted pastry wheel, or large chef's knife, cut between mounds to separate rectangle into equal-sized squares. Leave on towel to dry.

FRESH, STUFFED PASTA
After leaving to dry for 1–2 hours, cook fresh, stuffed pasta immediately, or store in the refrigerator and cook within one day.

COOK & SERVE PASTA

39 PASTA PORTIONS

500 g (1 lb) fresh or dried pasta will serve six to eight as an appetizer, or four as a main course; use less pasta if the sauce is rich.

Stuffed or layered pasta made with shop-bought, dried pasta is heavier than fresh stuffed pasta, so serve smaller portions. The same applies to wholemeal pasta, which is more filling than the white-flour variety.

40 SAUCEPAN SIZE

Use a pan that is big enough to contain sufficient water for the quantity of pasta to be cooked, and to leave enough room for the pasta pieces to move around freely in the water without touching and sticking together.

CHOICE OF
PAN SIZES

41 PASTA-TO-WATER

Add salt to taste

Pasta	Water
250 g (½ lb)	3 litres (5 pints)
500 g (1 lb)	5 litres (8 pints)
750 g (1½ lb)	6 litres (10 pints)

42 FAST-BOIL PASTA

Pasta must be cooked in fast-boiling water. Bring the water to the boil before adding the pasta; cover the pot until the water comes back to the boil, then remove the lid.

STIR PASTA TO PREVENT STICKING

43 ADD PASTA TO WATER

When the water is boiling, add salt as required, then add the pasta. Stir immediately to prevent the pasta sticking to the pot or to itself and to ensure that it is totally immersed.

◁ LONG PASTA
Allow long sticks of pasta to curl into the water as they soften; do not break them.

HOME-MADE PASTA ▷
Drop home-made pasta straight into a pan of boiling water from the tea towel on which it was drying.

44 PASTA DRAINER

Cook small or finely cut pasta in a pasta drainer immersed in a pan of boiling water. When the pasta is cooked, simply lift out and drain.

COOKING SMALL PASTA

45 IS IT READY?

Cook pasta until it is slightly resistant when nipped with a thumb nail, or firm to the bite (*al dente*), with no hard centre or raw taste.

TEST WITH THUMB NAIL

46 DRAIN & RINSE

As soon as the pasta is ready, drain and rinse – in hot water if it is to be served hot, in cold if it is to be used in a salad or in a baked dish.

DRAIN IN COLANDER

47 SERVE HOT

Pasta cools down rapidly, so warm the serving bowl or individual plates, ready to serve the pasta as soon as it is cooked and drained.

SERVE IN WARM BOWL

48 TOSS QUICKLY

Toss hot, cooked pasta with the prepared sauce or dressing as soon as the pasta is ready. If left to stand, pasta tends to stick together.

COAT WITH SAUCE

49 PAN-FRY PASTA

Pan-fry uncooked fresh egg pasta (particularly string shapes) in hot oil to make a crisp brown cake, and serve with sauce. Alternatively, mix some cooked pasta with beaten egg and pan-fry it as a flat pancake.

50 DEEP-FRYING

Stuffed, oriental savouries, such as wontons and egg rolls, are usually deep-fried. You can use the same technique for stuffed Italian-style pasta such as cannelloni or ravioli. Cook in batches until golden brown. Drain on paper towels.

51 PREVENT STICKING

Pasta has a tendency to stick to the sides of the dish when baked. To prevent this, brush the dish with a little oil or melted butter. If the recipe includes a sauce, coat the sides of the dish with it before adding the pasta.

OIL BAKING DISH

52 AVOID A CRUST

To prevent pasta drying out and becoming crusty when baked, spread a thick layer of sauce on top, making sure that all of the pasta is well covered. Alternatively, tightly cover the top of the baking dish with a sheet of aluminium foil.

SAUCE TOPPING
Here, a top layer of tomato-cream sauce will help prevent the pasta drying out as it bakes.

53 PERFECT PARTNERS

Parmigiano-Reggiano cheese, more commonly known as Parmesan, is the perfect complement to many pasta dishes. Use it to flavour sauces or stuffings, or sprinkle it on top of cooked pasta. Although Parmesan is expensive, a little goes a long way.

FRESH IS BEST
Freshly grated Parmesan is far superior to the ready-grated variety in tubs and packets.

54 GARNISHES

Choose a garnish to complement the taste and enhance the appearance of a dish. Typical garnishes for pasta dishes include basil and parsley (chopped or sprigs), curls of Parmesan cheese, olives, capers, and mussels or clams.

SLICED OLIVES

PARSLEY

BASIL

CHERRY TOMATOES

◁ COMPLEMENTARY GARNISHES
The garnish of finely grated lemon zest echoes the dish's lemon sauce, while the green spring onion rings provide attractive colour contrast.

55 HOW TO EAT LONG PASTA

It is possible to eat long pasta elegantly if you follow this very simple technique:
- Pick up a few strands on the prongs of a fork.
- Hold the tip of the fork firmly against the side of the bowl, or in the hollow of a spoon held in the other hand.
- Twirl the fork around until the strands are all rolled onto it.

TWIRL SPAGHETTI ONTO FORK

PASTA SOUPS & SALADS

56 MINESTRONE SOUP
Serves 6–8 as appetizer or light lunch

Ingredients
*110 g (4 oz) haricot beans,
soaked overnight
2 carrots, diced
2 onions, diced
4 stalks celery, sliced
60 ml (4 tbsp) olive oil
3 litres (5¼ pints) chicken
or vegetable stock
1 bay leaf
2 leeks, sliced
12 green beans, cut in
1.25 cm (½ in) pieces
1 garlic clove, crushed
Salt and pepper
1 small cauliflower, divided
into florets
90 g (3 oz) ditalini
2 courgettes, cut in
1.25 cm (½ in) pieces
3 tomatoes, peeled, seeded,
and chopped
30 g (2 tbsp) chopped fresh
basil or parsley
110 g (4 oz) grated
Parmesan cheese*

- Simmer haricot beans until tender, approximately 2 hours. Take off heat and leave in liquid.
- Sauté diced carrots, onions, and celery in olive oil. Add chicken or vegetable stock, bay leaf, and haricot beans with their liquid, and bring to boil. Add sliced leeks, green beans, garlic, salt and pepper. Cover and simmer for 5 minutes. Add cauliflower florets and ditalini and cook until pasta is *al dente*, about 10 minutes. Add courgettes and tomatoes and simmer until tender, 5 minutes.
- Remove bay leaf; stir in chopped basil or parsley. Serve with Parmesan cheese.

57 VEGETABLE NOODLE SOUP

Serves 6–8 as appetizer or light lunch

Ingredients
500 g (1 lb) leeks
175 g (6 oz) turnips, diced
225 g (8 oz) carrots, diced
3 celery sticks, diced
*½ head white cabbage,
finely shredded*
*125 g (4 oz) French beans,
sliced*
2 garlic cloves, chopped
*2.5 litres (4 pints) chicken
stock*
Bouquet garni
Salt and pepper
*225 g (8 oz) courgettes,
diced*
*225 g (8 oz) tomatoes,
peeled, seeded, and chopped*
125 g (4 oz) vermicelli

- Trim leeks; slit each in half lengthwise, then wash thoroughly under cold running water to get rid of any grit. With sharp knife, cut each leek half crosswise into 5 mm (¼ in) slices.
- Put leeks, turnips, carrots, celery, cabbage, beans, and chopped garlic into large stockpot.
- Add chicken stock, bouquet garni, and salt and pepper. Bring to boil; cover, and simmer for 30 minutes. Add courgettes and tomatoes and simmer until tender, about 25 minutes longer.
- Stir in vermicelli and continue simmering until pasta is just tender, 4–5 minutes.

TO SERVE
*The soup is served here with
tomato-flavoured croûtes.*

58 FUSILLI & PESTO SALAD

Serves 6–8 as appetizer

Ingredients
60 g (2 oz) fresh basil
6 garlic cloves
45 g (1½ oz) pine nuts
125 g (4 oz) grated Parmesan
175 ml (6 fl oz) olive oil
Salt and pepper
500 g (1 lb) fusilli

1 Strip off basil leaves from stalks, reserving few sprigs for garnish; rinse and pat dry. Put in processor with garlic, pine nuts, and Parmesan.

2 Add 45 ml (3 tbsp) olive oil and process until smooth, scraping down bowl as necessary.

To Serve

Spoon the sauce-coated fusilli onto individual plates and garnish with the reserved sprigs of basil. Here, cherry tomatoes add bright contrast.

3 With blade turning, add remaining oil, pouring it in slowly so sauce emulsifies. When all oil has been added, scrape down sides of bowl and process again briefly. Season to taste with salt and pepper and transfer to mixing bowl. Cook fusilli in boiling salted water until *al dente*. Drain.

4 Rinse drained fusilli under cold running water. Drain thoroughly. Add to sauce in mixing bowl and toss together until pasta is well coated.

59 HOT PARSLEY PASTA SALAD

Serves 6 as appetizer

Ingredients
Pasta dough
225 g (8 oz) strong plain flour
2 eggs and 1 egg yolk
30 ml (2 tbsp) water
5 ml (1 tsp) salt

Medium bunch of flat parsley
Sprigs of flat parsley, chopped
20 ml (4 tsp) red wine vinegar
37.5 ml (2½ tbsp) soured cream
1 garlic clove, chopped
2 shallots, chopped
Salt and pepper
60 ml (4 tbsp) vegetable oil
2 hard-boiled eggs, shelled and sliced

1 Make pasta dough (see p.20), omitting oil and adding egg yolk and water in place of one egg. Knead until smooth and elastic. Roll into 13 cm (5 in) strips. Brush water over half of each pasta strip.

2 Pull leaves off flat parsley. Arrange leaves in rows about 2.5 cm (1 in) apart on dampened half of dough strip; fold other half over. Roll gently with rolling pin to seal layers together. Repeat process with remaining strips of pasta dough.

3 With pastry wheel or chef's knife cut dough, between rows of parsley leaves, into 2.5 cm (1 in) squares. Place squares on floured tea towel and sprinkle lightly with flour. Leave to dry, 1–2 hours.

4 Chop parsley sprigs, reserving few for garnish; whisk vinegar, cream, garlic, shallots, chopped parsley, salt and pepper until slightly thickened. Gradually add oil.

5 Cook pasta squares in boiling salted water until tender but still chewy. Drain; rinse with hot water; drain again. Add to dressing and toss gently to mix.

TO SERVE
Garnish with a slice of hard-boiled egg and a sprig of parsley.

60 FRESH TUNA PASTA SALAD NIÇOISE

Serves 6 as main course

Ingredients

Marinade and dressing
8 anchovy fillets, chopped
1 sprig of fresh thyme, chopped
2 garlic cloves, chopped
60 ml (4 tbsp) lemon juice
15 ml (1 tbsp) balsamic
vinegar
5 ml (1 tsp) Dijon mustard
Black pepper
250 ml (8 fl oz) olive oil

━

1 kg (2 lb) fresh tuna steaks, skinned and
cut into 2.5 cm (1 in) cubes
750 g (1½ lb) French beans
500 g (1 lb) farfalle
500 g (1 lb) cherry tomatoes

1 Make marinade: put anchovies, thyme, and garlic in bowl and mix. Add lemon juice, vinegar, mustard, and black pepper and whisk together. Slowly add olive oil, whisking until mixture emulsifies.

2 ▽ Thread tuna cubes onto skewers and place on large plate. Spoon about 5 tablespoons of marinade over kebabs and cover with clingfilm. Leave to marinate in refrigerator for at least 1 hour, turning skewers occasionally.

3 △ Top and tail French beans. Rinse, then cook in boiling salted water till tender but still firm. Drain beans, rinse under cold running water; drain. Place in bowl with 5 tablespoons of dressing.

4 Toss French beans with dressing; set aside. Cook farfalle. Drain well; rinse under cold water; drain. Put in bowl with 5 tablespoons of dressing; toss together.

5 Grill kebabs for 2 minutes; turn and baste with dressing, then grill for a further 2 minutes. Arrange on plates with farfalle, cherry tomatoes, and beans.

TO SERVE
Spoon the remaining dressing over each serving. If you wish, garnish with olives.

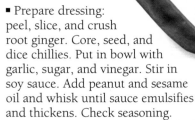

61 ASIAN NOODLE SALAD

Serves 4 as main course

Ingredients
Spicy soy dressing
2 cm (¾ in) piece of fresh root ginger
2 fresh green chillies
2 garlic cloves, peeled and chopped
10 ml (2 tsp) sugar
60 ml (4 tbsp) rice wine vinegar
125 ml (4 fl oz) soy sauce
60 ml (4 tbsp) peanut oil
30 ml (2 tbsp) sesame oil

═══

225 g (8 oz) fine dried egg noodles
175 g (6 oz) mangetout, trimmed
4 spring onions
75 g (2½ oz) roasted unsalted peanuts
Small bunch fresh coriander
375 g (12 oz) cooked peeled prawns
Salt and pepper

- Prepare dressing: peel, slice, and crush root ginger. Core, seed, and dice chillies. Put in bowl with garlic, sugar, and vinegar. Stir in soy sauce. Add peanut and sesame oil and whisk until sauce emulsifies and thickens. Check seasoning.
- Cook egg noodles in boiling salted water till tender but still chewy, 4–6 minutes, stirring occasionally. Drain noodles, rinse with hot water, and drain again thoroughly.
- Place noodles in large bowl; pour over dressing; toss until well coated. Set aside for at least 1 hour.
- Cook mangetout in boiling salted water until tender yet crisp, 2–3 minutes. Drain, rinse with running cold water, and drain again. Cut each pod diagonally into 2–3 slices.
- Cut spring onions crosswise into thin diagonal slices, including some green tops. Coarsely chop peanuts. Strip coriander leaves from stalks, and chop leaves coarsely.
- Add mangetout, sliced spring onions, two-thirds of peanuts and coriander, and all prawns to noodles. Toss thoroughly and season to taste.

TO SERVE
Garnish salad with remaining chopped peanuts and coarsely chopped coriander.

PASTA SAUCES

62 CLASSIC BECHAMEL SAUCE
Makes 250 ml (8 fl oz)

Ingredients
250 ml (8 fl oz) milk
22 g (¾ oz) butter
22 g (¾ oz) flour
Grated nutmeg
Salt and white pepper

Bring milk to boil in saucepan; set aside. In heavy saucepan, melt butter. Whisk in flour and cook until foaming, about 1 minute. Remove pan from heat and cool slightly. Strain milk through sieve and add to pan, whisking constantly. Return sauce to heat and bring to boil, whisking until sauce thickens. Season to taste with nutmeg, salt and pepper, and simmer for another 2 minutes.

63 FRESH TOMATO SAUCE
Makes 375 ml (12 fl oz)

Ingredients
45 ml (3 tbsp) vegetable oil
2 medium onions, finely
chopped
1 kg (2 lb) tomatoes,
chopped
3 garlic cloves, chopped
30 ml (2 tbsp) tomato purée
5 ml (1 tsp) sugar
Bouquet garni
Salt and pepper

1 In large pan heat oil; sauté onions till brown, stirring often. Add tomatoes, garlic, purée, sugar, and bouquet garni.

2 Cook tomato mixture until it is fairly thick, 12–15 minutes. Strain through sieve into bowl, pressing down with small ladle to extract all tomato pulp. Season to taste with salt and pepper.

64 PESTO SAUCE
For 500 g (1 lb) pasta

Ingredients
45 g (1½ oz) basil leaves, washed,
dried, and chopped
6 garlic cloves, peeled
40 g (1½ oz) pine nuts
125 g (4 oz) grated Parmesan cheese
175 ml (6 fl oz) olive oil
Salt and pepper

1 Place chopped basil leaves, garlic, pine nuts, and Parmesan cheese in mortar. Pound with pestle to combine.

2 When basil and Parmesan mixture forms smooth purée, gradually add olive oil. Continue pounding until oil is incorporated and sauce is well blended.

3 Before serving Pesto sauce, season to taste with salt and pepper. (If you like, purée ingredients in food processor, adding olive oil with blade turning.)

65 FREEZE PESTO PORTIONS

Pesto freezes well, without any loss of flavour or colour. Make double or triple quantities of recipe and freeze the extra in an ice-cube tray for single-serving portions. Toss a portion with hot spaghetti for a quick individual snack, or stir into vegetable soup for added flavour.

66 CARBONARA

For 500 g (1 lb) pasta

Ingredients
30 g (1 oz) butter
2 garlic cloves, peeled and chopped
225 g (8 oz) sliced pancetta or smoked bacon, cut into strips
60 ml (4 tbsp) dry white wine
4 eggs
90 g (3 oz) grated Parmesan cheese
Salt and pepper
Sprigs of parsley

■ Melt butter in frying pan; gently sauté garlic and sliced pancetta or bacon for 1–2 minutes. Add white wine and continue cooking till it is reduced by half. Remove frying pan from heat and keep mixture warm.

FRESH BROWN EGGS

TO SERVE
Carbonara is served here with fettuccine, sprinkled with freshly ground black pepper.

■ Put eggs and Parmesan cheese in large bowl. Season lightly with salt and pepper and beat well with fork. Finely chop sprigs of parsley.
■ Add hot, cooked pasta to egg and Parmesan mixture in bowl and toss quickly. Add pancetta mixture and chopped parsley. Toss together and serve immediately on warm plates.

67 SERVING CARBONARA SAUCE

The eggs in Carbonara sauce (*see above*) are not cooked, but just lightly set by the heat of the cooked pasta. It is essential, therefore, that the pasta is added as soon as it has been drained, rinsed with hot water, and drained again. Toss together, and serve immediately on hot plates.

68 EGG & ANCHOVY
For 500 g (1 lb) pasta

Ingredients
4 anchovy fillets
125 g (4 oz) mozzarella cheese
3 egg yolks
75 g (2½ oz) butter, cut in pieces

Chop anchovy fillets and mozzarella cheese. Lightly beat egg yolks and combine with anchovies and cheese in serving bowl. Toss with butter and hot, cooked pasta of choice.

69 GORGONZOLA
For 500 g (1 lb) pasta

Ingredients
125 g (4 oz) Gorgonzola cheese
125 ml (4 fl oz) double cream
30 g (1 oz) butter
30 g (1 oz) grated Parmesan cheese

Crumble Gorgonzola cheese into pan with double cream and butter; stir over low heat until smooth. Toss with freshly grated Parmesan cheese and hot, cooked pasta.

70 SEAFOOD SAUCE
For 500 g (1 lb) pasta

Ingredients
60 ml (4 tbsp) olive oil
1 onion, chopped
1 carrot, chopped
2 garlic cloves, chopped
125 g (4 oz) mushrooms, sliced
Salt and pepper
60 ml (4 tbsp) dry white wine
2 plum tomatoes, peeled, seeded, and chopped
500 g (1 lb) prawns, shelled
1 kg (2 lb) mussels or clams, steamed open and shelled; reserve cooking liquid
45 g (3 tbsp) chopped parsley

- Heat olive oil in sauté pan and cook onion and carrot until soft. Add chopped garlic cloves, sliced mushrooms, and salt and pepper to taste. Mix ingredients together.
- Lower heat and cook until all liquid in pan has evaporated, 2–3 minutes. Pour in wine and cook for 4–5 minutes to reduce sauce. Add chopped tomatoes and simmer for another 5–7 minutes.
- Add prawns and simmer for 1–2 minutes. Add mussels or clams with 250 ml (8 fl oz) of their cooking liquid, strained. Add chopped parsley, and check and adjust seasoning.
- Serve with spaghetti.

71 TOMATO & BASIL SAUCE

For 500 g (1 lb) pasta

Ingredients
Large bunch fresh basil
1 garlic clove
900 g (2 lb) large, ripe
tomatoes
125 ml (4 fl oz) extra-virgin
olive oil
Salt and pepper

- Strip basil leaves from stalks and chop coarsely. Finely chop garlic. Chop tomatoes, without peeling or seeding them.
- Place basil, garlic, and tomatoes in bowl and add olive oil. Stir to combine. Season to taste with salt and pepper. Serve with hot, cooked fettuccine.

TO SERVE
Sprinkle freshly grated Parmesan cheese over Tomato & Basil Sauce, which is served here with fettuccine.

72 ANCHOVY, OLIVE, & CAPER SAUCE

For 375 g (12 oz) pasta

Ingredients
3 garlic cloves
1 dried red chilli pepper
6 anchovy fillets
500 g (1 lb) tomatoes
90 ml (3 fl oz) olive oil
125 g (4 oz) large black
olives, stoned
1 tbsp capers
Salt

- Finely chop garlic; chop red chilli pepper and anchovy fillets; peel, seed, and chop tomatoes.
- Heat oil in frying pan and fry garlic and chilli pepper until garlic starts to brown. Add chopped anchovy fillets and mash with fork.
- Add tomatoes, olives, and capers to mixture in frying pan and stir well. Season to taste with salt. Continue simmering while pasta is cooking.
- Serve with hot, cooked spaghetti.

73 SPICY TOMATO & BACON
For 500 g (1 lb) pasta

Ingredients
1.4 kg (3 lb) plum tomatoes
1 fresh red chilli pepper
375 g (12 oz) mushrooms
5–7 sprigs fresh oregano
125 g (4 oz) thick-cut bacon
rashers
2 garlic cloves
Salt and pepper

- Peel, seed, and chop tomatoes coarsely. Cut fresh red chilli pepper lengthwise in half; remove core and fleshy white ribs, and scrape out seeds; dice finely.
- Wipe mushrooms with dampened paper towels and trim stalks. Place mushrooms stalk-side down and slice across. Strip oregano leaves from stalks, reserving few leaves for garnish; chop leaves finely. Stack bacon rashers on chopping board and cut across into wide strips. Peel and finely chop garlic cloves.
- In frying pan, fry bacon over low heat, stirring occasionally, until browned, 5–7 minutes. Spoon off fat, leaving about 45 ml (3 tbsp) in which to sauté sliced mushrooms. Increase heat; add mushrooms to frying pan. Cook until mushrooms

TO SERVE
Sprinkle freshly grated Parmesan cheese over each serving and garnish with oregano

are softened and most of liquid has evaporated, stirring with wooden spoon to prevent sticking.
- Add chopped tomatoes with their juice to mushrooms in frying pan, together with garlic, chilli pepper, oregano, salt and pepper. Bring to boil, cover with lid, and simmer, stirring occasionally until sauce is thick and rich, 25–30 minutes.
- If sauce needs thickening cook, without lid, for a few minutes more.
- Check sauce for seasoning. Pour sauce over hot, cooked pasta and toss together. Serve immediately.

74 PRIMAVERA SAUCE

For 500 g (1 lb) pasta

Ingredients

2 medium courgettes
Salt and pepper
2 medium carrots
200 g (7 oz) shelled peas
45 g (1½ oz) butter
*175 ml (6 fl oz) double
cream*
*30 g (1 oz) grated
Parmesan cheese*

TO SERVE ▽
*Primavera is served here
with spaghetti and a baked
courgette fan garnish.*

▪ Trim ends of courgettes and cut each in half lengthwise. Cut each half lengthwise in half again. Next, cut courgette lengths into 9 mm (⅜ in) chunks. Simmer in boiling salted water until barely tender, 2–3 minutes. Drain in colander, rinse with cold water, then drain again thoroughly. Set courgettes aside until required.

▪ Peel and trim ends of carrots; cut into chunks of a similar size to courgettes. Place in saucepan and cover with cold water; add salt, and bring to boil. Simmer until just tender, 8–10 minutes. Drain in colander, rinse with cold water, then drain thoroughly. Set carrots aside until required.

▪ Bring small saucepan of salted water to boil. Add peas and simmer until tender, 3–8 minutes. Drain, rinse with cold water, and drain again thoroughly. Set peas aside until they are required.

▪ Heat butter in large pan; add courgette and carrot chunks and peas and sauté for 1 minute. Add cream, stir well to mix, and heat until mixture is simmering. Remove pan from heat, add cooked, drained pasta and toss to mix with cream vegetable mixture. Add freshly grated Parmesan cheese and toss gently to combine.

75 RAGU BOLOGNESE
For 500 g (1 lb) pasta

Ingredients
60 ml (4 tbsp) vegetable oil
2 onions, chopped
2 garlic cloves, chopped
1 medium carrot, diced
375 g (12 oz) minced beef
375 g (12 oz) minced pork
250 ml (8 fl oz) milk
375 ml (12 fl oz) dry
white wine
1 kg (2 lb) tomatoes
15 ml (1 tbsp) tomato purée
Bouquet garni
Salt and pepper
500 ml (16 fl oz) water

TO SERVE △
*Ragù Bolognese is served here with its
classic partner, spaghetti, and sprinkled
liberally with Parmesan cheese.*

1 Heat vegetable oil in sauté pan, add chopped onions, chopped garlic, and diced carrot, and sauté until soft, stirring frequently. Add minced beef and minced pork and cook until they lose their pink colour. Add milk, stir, then simmer until liquid has evaporated. Add white wine and simmer until it also has evaporated.

2 Peel, seed, and coarsely chop tomatoes. Add to meat mixture in sauté pan with any juice. Add tomato purée, bouquet garni, salt and pepper to taste, and water. Simmer until sauce is thick, 1½–2 hours, stirring occasionally. Add a little water if sauce starts to stick. Discard bouquet garni and check seasoning before serving.

76 BUTTER & CREAM SAUCE
For 500 g (1 lb) pasta

Ingredients
60 g (2 oz) butter
*250 ml (8 fl oz) double
cream*
*60 g (2 oz) Parmesan
cheese*

TO SERVE
*Serve with freshly ground
black pepper and grated
Parmesan cheese.*

■ In large pan, cook pasta of choice in boiling salted water; when ready, drain well and return to pan. Meanwhile, in small pan, melt butter, add double cream and bring almost to boil. Pour over hot, cooked pasta in large pan, and toss gently over low heat until pasta is coated with sauce.

■ Add freshly grated Parmesan cheese to pasta mixture and continue tossing over low heat until mixture is very hot. Check and adjust seasoning.

■ Serve at once on warmed plates.

77 WHITE CLAM SAUCE
For 500 g (1 lb) pasta

Ingredients
3.6 kg (8 lb) clams
1 onion, finely chopped
250 ml (8 fl oz) dry white wine

2 garlic cloves, finely chopped
60 ml (4 tbsp) olive oil
Sprigs of parsley, chopped
Salt and pepper

TO SERVE
*Garnish, as
here, with clams in
shells and sprigs of parsley.*

1 Scrub clams; put in large pan with onion and wine. Cook until shells open; discard any unopened clams.

2 Remove clams from pan, reserving liquid. When cool, take clams from shells; reserve a few in shells for garnish.

3 Reduce clam cooking liquid over high heat until only about 250 ml (8 fl oz) remains. Strain cooking liquid into small bowl through fine sieve. Sauté garlic in oil for 30 seconds, being careful not to burn; add shelled clams, chopped parsley, and reduced cooking liquid, and stir to mix. Season to taste with salt and pepper. Serve with spinach linguine. Garnish with a few clams in their shells.

78 RED CLAM SAUCE
For 500 g (1 lb) pasta

Ingredients
As for White Clam Sauce
1 kg (2 lb) tomatoes

Follow Steps 1 and 2 of recipe for White Clam Sauce. Peel, seed, and chop tomatoes. Add at Step 3, after sautéing garlic. Simmer till mixture thickens, stirring occasionally. Add clams, cooking liquid, and parsley.

SERVE WITH SPINACH LINGUINE

51

79 OLIVE OIL & GARLIC DRESSING
For 500 g (1 lb) pasta

Ingredients
4 garlic cloves
125 ml (4 fl oz) olive oil
Salt and pepper

Finely chop garlic cloves. Heat garlic in olive oil until golden brown, being careful not to burn it. Season with salt and pepper. Serve with long, thin pasta such as cappellini or spaghettini.

80 THREE CHEESES
For 500 g (1 lb) pasta

Ingredients
125 g (4 oz) Gorgonzola cheese
175 ml (6 fl oz) double cream
60 g (2 oz) freshly grated
Parmesan cheese
125 g (4 oz) ricotta cheese

ADD RICOTTA CHEESE

TO SERVE
Toss sauce with fresh fettuccine.

Remove rind from Gorgonzola cheese; chop into fairly small pieces. Place in saucepan with cream, Parmesan cheese, and ricotta cheese. Heat gently, stirring all the time, until all three cheeses are melted. Be careful not to overheat sauce.

81 CHOOSING & COOKING CHEESE
Hard cheeses such as Gruyère and Parmesan can withstand higher temperatures, so are a good choice for cooking. When adding grated cheese to a sauce, heat until just melted: never boil or reheat.

STUFFED & BAKED PASTA

82 MEAT FILLING
For 375 g (12 oz) pasta

Ingredients
45 g (1½ oz) butter
1 small onion, finely chopped
2 carrots, finely chopped
1 celery stalk, finely chopped
15 g (½ oz) dried mushrooms, soaked and chopped
500 g (1 lb) minced lean beef
125 ml (4 fl oz) Marsala
30 ml (2 tbsp) tomato purée

▪ Melt butter in frying pan. Sauté onion, carrots, and celery until soft. Add mushrooms (reserving soaking liquid) and beef. Cook until minced beef loses pink colour, 4–5 minutes.
▪ Add Marsala to meat mixture and boil until liquid has evaporated. Add tomato purée dissolved in some of mushroom soaking liquid. Stir and cover pan. Simmer for 1 hour, stirring occasionally. If mixture begins to stick, add a little water.
▪ Cool before using to stuff small pasta shapes.

83 CHEESE FILLING
For 375 g (12 oz) pasta

Ingredients
1 kg (2 lb) spinach, cooked, squeezed dry, and chopped
60 g (2 oz) butter
250 g (½ lb) ricotta cheese
Ground nutmeg
Salt and pepper

▪ Sauté cooked, chopped spinach in butter. Leave to cool slightly then mix with ricotta cheese and pinch of ground nutmeg. Season mixture to taste with salt and pepper. Let cool before using to stuff shapes such as tortellini or lunette.

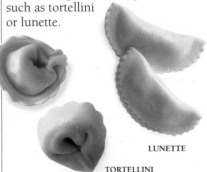

LUNETTE

TORTELLINI

84 SPINACH & CHEESE PINWHEELS

Serves 6 as main course

Ingredients

500 g (1 lb) Fresh egg pasta dough
(see p.20)

━━

Spinach filling
450 g (15 oz) frozen leaf spinach
225 g (8 oz) fresh goat cheese
30 g (1 oz) butter
225 g (8 oz) ricotta cheese
Ground nutmeg
2 eggs, lightly beaten
Salt and pepper

Topping
60 g (2 oz) butter
60 ml (4 tbsp) double cream

━━

Red pepper sauce
750 g (1½ lb) red peppers
Small bunch fresh basil
30 ml (2 tbsp) olive oil
500 g (1 lb) tomatoes, peeled, seeded,
and chopped
1 garlic clove, chopped
2 spring onions, chopped

1 Knead and roll out pasta dough; leave to dry until leathery. Cut dough into 10 x 20 cm (4 x 8 in) rectangles. Spread on tea towel; sprinkle with a little flour. Leave to dry, 1–2 hours. Meanwhile cook spinach, drain thoroughly, and squeeze with hands to remove excess moisture. With knife, finely chop spinach. Crumble goat cheese, discarding any rind.

2 Gently melt butter in frying pan; add spinach; cook until all moisture has evaporated. Allow to cool slightly, then stir in ricotta and goat cheese, pinch of nutmeg, and salt and pepper to taste. Add eggs and mix well. Cook pasta rectangles in boiling salted water until barely tender. Drain, place in bowl of cold water, then drain again thoroughly.

3 Preheat oven to 190° C/375° F/gas 5. Spread 45–60 ml (3–4 tbsp) spinach filling on each pasta rectangle, leaving narrow border. Roll rectangles up from short end and arrange in buttered baking dish. For topping, melt butter, mix with double cream and pour over rolls. Cover baking dish with buttered foil and bake in preheated oven until skewer inserted in pasta roll in centre of dish is hot to touch when removed, about 30 minutes.

4 Grill whole red peppers on rack about 10 cm (4 in) from heat, until skin is black and blistered. Place in plastic bag, close, and leave until peppers are cool enough to handle. With table knife, peel skin; remove core; halve each pepper and scrape away seeds. Rinse under running water and pat dry. Cut into chunks. Chop basil leaves, reserving few sprigs.

5 Heat olive oil in frying pan; add roast pepper chunks, chopped tomatoes, garlic, spring onions, and basil. Cook until mixture thickens; stir occasionally. Purée sauce in processor until almost smooth. Season with salt and pepper.

TO SERVE
Cut rolls diagonally into slices. Spoon some sauce onto each plate; arrange pinwheels on top. Garnish with reserved basil sprigs.

85 CHEESE TORTELLINI WITH SMOKED SALMON
Serves 6–8 as appetizer or main course

Ingredients

Filling

150 g (5 oz) mozzarella cheese
300 g (10 oz) ricotta cheese
30 g (1 oz) grated Parmesan cheese
Ground nutmeg
Salt and pepper
1 egg

Topping

125 g (4 oz) smoked salmon
Small bunch fresh dill
60 g (2 oz) butter
250 ml (8 fl oz) double cream

500 g (1 lb) Fresh egg pasta dough
(see p.20)

1 Cut mozzarella cheese into cubes and place in large bowl. Add ricotta cheese and grated Parmesan cheese and mix well. Add pinch of ground nutmeg and season to taste with salt and pepper.

2 Lightly beat egg and combine with cheeses in bowl. Cut smoked salmon into strips. Chop dill, reserving few sprigs for garnish. Roll out dough and cut into rounds with 6 cm (2½ in) pastry cutter.

3 Using pastry brush or fingers, lightly moisten edge of each pasta round with water. Place 1 teaspoonful cheese filling onto centre of each round. Fold one side over to enclose filling. Pinch edges together with fingers. Gently curve around finger, turning sealed edge up to form upward-curved pleat.

4 Pinch together pointed ends of stuffed pasta round to form ring. Stuff, seal, and shape remaining pasta dough rounds. Spread out completed tortellini on floured tea towel and sprinkle lightly with flour or fine cornmeal. Leave to dry, 1–2 hours.

5 Cook tortellini in boiling salted water until tender but still chewy, stirring occasionally to prevent sticking. Drain in colander, rinse with hot water, and drain again thoroughly. Meanwhile, gently heat butter in saucepan until melted.

6 Add tortellini to saucepan and gently toss until all are evenly coated with butter. Add cream, smoked salmon, and chopped dill. Toss over moderate heat until ingredients are thoroughly heated.

TO SERVE
Serve tortellini on warmed serving dish and garnish with reserved sprigs of dill.

86 PREVENT TORTELLINI BURSTING

To prevent stuffed pasta such as tortellini bursting while they are cooking, be careful not to overfill the pasta rounds. Seal the edges of each piece by first moistening with water, then pinching together.

87 AUBERGINE LASAGNE WITH CHEESE SAUCE
Serves 8 as main course

Ingredients
Spinach pasta dough
*90 g (3 oz) fresh spinach, cooked, drained,
squeezed dry, and finely chopped*
300 g (10 oz) strong plain flour
3 eggs
15 ml (1 tbsp) vegetable oil
5 ml (1 tsp) salt
Oil for baking dish

==

Filling
500 g (1 lb) aubergines
Vegetable oil for brushing aubergines
500 g (1 lb) tomatoes
250 g (8 oz) mozzarella cheese

==

Cheese sauce
1 litre (1⅔ pints) milk
90 g (3 oz) butter
45 g (1½ oz) flour
Ground nutmeg
Salt and pepper
125 g (4 oz) grated Parmesan cheese

1 Make pasta dough (*see p.20*), adding spinach along with eggs, oil, and salt. Knead and roll out dough, then leave to dry, 5–10 minutes. Cut into 10 x 20 cm (4 x 8 in) rectangles; spread on floured te towel and sprinkle with flour; leave to dry, 1–2 hours. Cook in boiling salted water until barely tender, 3–5 minutes. Transfer pasta to bowl of cold water to stop cooking; remove with slotted spoon and drain thoroughly on clean tea towel.

2 Trim aubergines; slice thickly. Place in colander, sprinkle with salt, and leave 30 minutes to draw out juices. Heat oven to 180° C/350° F/gas 4. Rinse aubergine slices and pat dry with paper towel. Place on oiled baking sheets and brush with oil. Bake in preheated oven until tender, turning once, 20–25 minutes. Core and slice tomatoes. Cut mozzarella cheese into 5 mm (¼ in) thick slices.

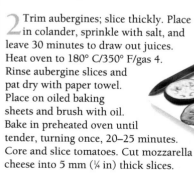

3 Scald milk in medium saucepan. Melt butter in another pan; whisk in flour, and cook for 1–2 minutes. Remove from heat and whisk in scalded milk. Return to heat and cook, whisking, until sauce boils and thickens. Season sauce with pinch of nutmeg and salt and pepper; simmer for 2 minutes. Remove from heat and stir in three-quarters of Parmesan cheese.

4 Preheat oven to 180° C/350° F/gas 4. Oil 23 x 32.5 cm (9 x 13 in) baking dish. Cover bottom with layer of cheese sauce then layer of pasta. Arrange half of aubergine slices on top; cover with sauce then another layer of pasta. Place half of mozzarella slices on top of pasta then half of tomato slices. Cover with another layer of pasta topped with aubergine slices.

5 Spoon over another layer of cheese sauce; top with pasta, another layer of mozzarella cheese and tomato slices and cover all with thick final layer of cheese sauce. Sprinkle with remaining Parmesan cheese and bake in oven, 30–45 minutes.

To Serve
When lasagne is bubbling and brown, cut into eight pieces and serve on warm plates.

88 LASAGNE BOLOGNESE

Serves 6–8 as main course

Ingredients

Bolognese sauce
750 g (1½ lb) tomatoes
2 tbsp finely chopped onion
2 tbsp finely chopped carrot
2 tbsp finely chopped celery
45 ml (1½ fl oz) olive oil
45 g (1½ oz) butter
500 g (1 lb) minced beef
250 ml (8 fl oz) white wine
125 ml (4 fl oz) milk
Ground nutmeg
Salt and pepper

=

500 g (1 lb) Fresh egg pasta dough (see p.20)
1 litre (1¾ pints) Classic béchamel sauce (see p.41)
Freshly grated Parmesan cheese
30 g (1 oz) butter

- Make Bolognese sauce: seed and coarsely chop tomatoes. Sauté onion, carrot, and celery in olive oil and butter till soft. Add minced beef and cook, stirring, until meat loses pink colour. Add wine; cook over medium heat until liquid evaporates. Pour in milk with pinch of nutmeg and cook till liquid evaporates. Stir in chopped tomatoes, with their juice. Simmer 3–4 hours, stirring occasionally. Season to taste at end of cooking time.
- Knead and roll out pasta dough; leave to dry, 5–10 minutes. Cut dough into 10 x 20 (4 x 8 in) rectangles. Spread on floured tea towel, sprinkle with flour, and leave to dry, 1–2 hours.
- Preheat oven to 180° C/350° F/gas 4. Butter 23 x 33 cm (9 x 13 in) baking dish. Cook pasta in boiling salted water until just tender. Transfer to bowl of cold water, then drain thoroughly.
- Spoon layer of Bolognese sauce over bottom of baking dish followed by layer of Béchamel sauce, sprinkled with Parmesan cheese. Top with layer of pasta rectangles then spread another layer of Bolognese sauce, topped with pasta. Spoon over another layer of Béchamel sauce, then sprinkle with more freshly grated Parmesan cheese.
- Continue layering until dish is nearly full. Finish with layer of Bolognese sauce topped with final thick layer of Béchamel sauce and sprinkling of Parmesan cheese. Dot top with butter. Bake until very hot and top is golden brown and bubbling, 30-40 minutes.
- Leave to rest for 5 minutes before cutting into portions. Serve on warmed plates.

89 MACARONI WITH FENNEL & RAISINS

Serves 4–6 as main course

Ingredients

500 g (1 lb) fennel bulbs
Salt and pepper
45 g (1½ oz) pine nuts
2 medium onions, thinly sliced
125 ml (4 fl oz) olive oil
45 g (1½ oz) raisins
500 g (1 lb) ricotta cheese
375 g (12 oz) macaroni
250 g (8 oz) mozzarella cheese, sliced

TO SERVE
Serve macaroni on warmed plates. If you like, garnish with chopped fennel leaves.

- Trim fennel bulbs; cut lengthwise in half, then slice crosswise. Cook in boiling salted water until just tender. Drain, reserving cooking liquid. Allow to cool then chop coarsely. Preheat oven to 190° C/375° F/gas 5; spread out pine nuts on baking sheet; bake until golden brown.
- In frying pan, sauté onions in oil until soft; add fennel, raisins, and pine nuts and stir. Take pan off heat and, when mixture is cool, stir in ricotta.
- In large pan, bring fennel cooking liquid, plus extra water if required, to boil; cook macaroni and drain. Preheat oven to 180° C/350 °F/gas 4.
- Place half of macaroni in buttered baking dish; top with half of ricotta mixture. Repeat layers of macaroni and ricotta topping. Place mozzarella cheese slices evenly over top of macaroni. Bake until cheese is melted and golden brown, and macaroni is very hot, 15–20 minutes.

90 RAVIOLI WITH SAFFRON RICOTTA

Serves 4 as main course

Ingredients
*500 g (1 lb) Fresh egg
pasta dough (see p.20)
¼ tsp saffron
15 ml (1 tbsp) milk
375 g (12 oz) ricotta cheese
Grated rind of 1 orange
1 egg
Nutmeg
Salt and pepper
125 g (4 oz) butter
Sage or rosemary leaves*

- Make dough and leave to rest for 1 hour. Divide dough in two and roll out thinly into two rectangles of equal size. Soak saffron in milk for 20 minutes, then mix into ricotta, along with orange rind, lightly beaten egg, pinch of grated nutmeg, and salt and pepper to taste. Place teaspoonfuls of ricotta stuffing on one sheet of pasta, in rows approximately 3.5 cm (1½ in) apart.
- Place second pasta rectangle on top and press down lightly with fingers between rows of filling. Cut between rows with pastry wheel or sharp knife to form squares of ravioli. Press firmly with fingertips around edges of ravioli, making certain that they are well sealed. Leave to dry on floured tea towel for 1–2 hours.
- Bring large pan of salted water to boil. Cook ravioli until they puff up slightly, 5 minutes. Meanwhile, melt butter and flavour with whole sage or chopped rosemary leaves.
- Drain ravioli carefully and toss in flavoured butter until well coated.

91 DELICATE PASTAS

Small stuffed pastas, such as ravioli and tortellini, are delicate to work with. To help prevent them breaking open or sticking to each other during cooking, freeze them first: after stuffing, dry for 1 hour, then lay in single layer on a floured baking sheet. Freeze until solid, about 1 hour, then cook as directed.

DRY ON FLOURED SURFACE

92 CANNELLONI WITH CHICKEN & MOZZARELLA

Serves 6–8 as main course

Ingredients

*500 g (1 lb) Fresh egg
pasta dough (see p.20)*
*375 g (12 oz) cooked
chicken breast, shredded*
*125 g (4 oz) mozzarella
cheese, cubed*
2 eggs, lightly beaten
Salt and pepper
6 thin slices pancetta

—

*375 ml (12 fl oz) Fresh
tomato sauce (see p.41)*
*30 g (2 tbsp) chopped fresh
basil leaves*
*30 g (1 oz) grated
Parmesan cheese*

■ Roll out dough thinly; trim edges and cut into 10 x 7.5 cm (4 x 3 in) rectangles. Spread out on tea towel and sprinkle with flour. Leave to dry, 1–2 hours. Cook pasta rectangles in boiling, salted water until barely tender, stirring gently to prevent sticking. Transfer to bowl of cold water. Remove and drain thoroughly on tea towel.

■ Place chicken, mozzarella cubes, and eggs in bowl. Add salt and pepper to taste. Mix well.

■ Preheat oven to 200° C/400° F/gas 6. Cut each slice of pancetta into four strips, discarding any bone or rind. Place one strip on each rectangle. Place 2–3 tablespoons filling onto each rectangle, along one long edge. Butter or oil large baking dish. Roll up each rectangle into a cylinder and arrange in baking dish, seam side down.

■ Add basil to tomato sauce and spoon over cannelloni in baking dish. Bake in heated oven until bubbling, 20–25 minutes.

TO SERVE
Sprinkle with Parmesan cheese and, if you like, garnish with basil leaves.

93 BAKED RIGATONI WITH MEATBALLS

Serves 6–8 as main course

Ingredients

1.4 kg (3 lb) fresh plum tomatoes, peeled,
seeded, and chopped
3 garlic cloves, finely chopped
Medium bunch fresh basil, chopped
Salt and pepper

—

Meatballs
500 g (1 lb) lean minced beef
125 g (4 oz) grated Parmesan cheese
3–5 sprigs flat-leaf parsley,
chopped
Juice of ½ lemon
Salt and pepper
1 egg
45 ml (3 tbsp) olive oil, plus more for
soufflé dish

—

375 g (12 oz) rigatoni

1 Put tomatoes, with any juice, in frying pan with two-thirds of chopped garlic and basil leaves. Cook over medium heat until mixture is slightly thickened, 10–12 minutes, stirring occasionally. Transfer mixture to food processor and process till smooth. Season to taste with salt and pepper; set aside. Wipe frying pan clean.

2 Put beef, quarter of Parmesan cheese, parsley, remaining garlic, lemon juice, and salt and pepper in bowl. Add egg and mix well. With wet hands, shape into balls 2 cm (¾ in) in diameter. Heat olive oil in frying pan and fry meatballs briskly, turning with knife, until brown on outside and still pink inside, 2–4 minutes. Transfer to large plate.

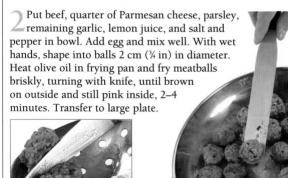

CHECK READINESS

FRY IN BATCHES

3 Preheat oven to 190° C/375° F/gas 5. Brush inside of 2 litre (3 pint) soufflé dish with oil. Cook pasta in boiling salted water until *al dente*, 8–10 minutes, stirring occasionally to prevent sticking. Drain thoroughly. Return pasta to pan and pour in tomato-basil sauce. Toss pasta and sauce together until pasta is well coated.

4 Spoon about one-third of rigatoni and sauce mixture into soufflé dish and level surface. Place half of fried meatballs on top. Sprinkle with about 1 tablespoon Parmesan cheese. Add half of remaining pasta and sauce, then rest of meatballs.

5 Sprinkle top with another tablespoon of Parmesan. Add rest of pasta and cover with remainder of Parmesan cheese. Bake in oven until very hot and top is browned, 30–40 minutes. Leave to stand till flavours blend, about 15 minutes.

TO SERVE
Sprinkle with grated Parmesan cheese; if you like, garnish with shredded basil.

94 CHINESE MOONS WITH LEMON SAUCE

Serves 8–10 as appetizer

Ingredients

175 g (6 oz) peeled cooked prawns
125 g (4 oz) Chinese leaves
1 lemon
2.5 cm (1 in) piece fresh root ginger
15 ml (1 tbsp) vegetable oil
1 garlic clove, chopped
1 shallot, chopped
5 ml (1 tsp) sherry
15 ml (1 tbsp) soy sauce

▬

500 g (1 lb) Fresh egg pasta dough
(see p.20)

Lemon sauce
2 lemons
45 g (1½ oz) butter
75 ml (2½ fl oz) double cream

1 Prepare prawn filling: coarsely chop prawns; set aside. With sharp knife, remove core of Chinese leaves and finely shred leaves. Discard any thick ribs. Rinse leaves under running cold water. Bring pan of salted water to boil, add Chinese leaves, and simmer until barely tender. Drain in colander, rinse with cold water, and drain again thoroughly. Grate zest from lemon with fine grater; set aside.

2 Peel and finely chop root ginger. Heat oil in frying pan and add shredded Chinese leaves, chopped garlic, shallot, and ginger. Sauté mixture for about 3 minutes, stirring frequently. Add prawns, lemon zest, sherry, and soy sauce and stir well. Taste filling to check seasoning. Process mixture in food processor until coarsely chopped or, if you prefer, chop finely with sharp knife.

3 On floured surface, knead and roll out pasta dough to thickness of postcard. With pastry cutter, cut out 7.5 cm (3 in) rounds. Spoon 1 teaspoonful filling onto centre of each round. Lightly brush around edge with water. Fold one side of pasta round over to enclose filling. Seal carefully by pinching edges together securely with fingertips. Repeat filling and sealing with all remaining dough rounds.

4 Spread filled pasta moons on floured tea towel; sprinkle with flour. Leave to dry, 1–2 hours. Meanwhile, prepare lemon sauce: grate zest from lemons, using finest side of grater. Melt butter in small pan; add double cream and half of lemon zest; stir. Keep warm while cooking pasta moons.

5 Cook pasta moons in boiling salted water until edges are tender but still chewy, 2–3 minutes. Stir occasionally to prevent sticking. Drain in colander, rinse with hot water, then drain thoroughly. Arrange on warmed individual plates.

To Serve

Spoon lemon sauce over pasta moons and sprinkle with lemon zest. If you like, add some finely sliced green spring onion.

STORE & REHEAT PASTA

95 STORE DRY PASTA

Thoroughly dry home-made pasta; sprinkle with flour and store in an airtight container for three to four days (egg pasta) or up to one week (eggless pasta). Shop-bought dried pasta will last for about two years.

AIRTIGHT JARS
Store dried pasta in sealed jars in a cool, dry place.

96 FRESH PASTA STORAGE

Place home-made filled pasta on a baking tray, dust lightly with flour, and refrigerate for up to one day. Or open-freeze on a tray, pack in plastic bags, and freeze for two months. Follow maker's guidelines for storing shop-bought fresh pasta.

FREEZE STUFFED PASTA

97 PREPARE & STORE PASTA SALAD

Whether intended as a side salad or appetizer, or a substantial main-course meal, a pasta salad can be made up to one day ahead. Toss the ingredients and dressing while the pasta is warm so that it absorbs the flavourings fully. Cover the salad and store in the refrigerator until required. Serve chilled, or bring to room temperature before serving.

98 FREEZE SAUCES

Pasta sauces that are based on cream, milk, or cheese do not freeze well, as such ingredients tend to separate when frozen. Tomato sauces, on the other hand, freeze particularly well, as do Pesto and Ragù Bolognese. Stuffed and layered pasta dishes that incorporate sauces, such as lasagne and cannelloni, will also freeze and reheat satisfactorily.

FREEZE SAUCE IN PLASTIC BAG

99 DEFROST WELL

Defrost frozen pasta sauces and prepared pasta dishes at room temperature or, more slowly, in the refrigerator. Alternatively, you can use a microwave oven to speed up the process, following the guidelines supplied with your particular oven.

100 REFRIGERATE

If you wish to prepare a pasta sauce ahead of time, or have some sauce left over, store it in an airtight container in the refrigerator for up to one day. Uncooked, stuffed pasta, such as ravioli, can also be kept in the refrigerator for one day.

101 REHEAT PASTA

Reheat, until bubbling, pasta sauces that have been stored in the refrigerator or frozen then defrosted. Stir gently to ensure that the ingredients are mixed. Layered pasta dishes reheat very well in a microwave oven.

REHEAT LAYERED PASTA
You can prepare layered pasta dishes up to 24 hours ahead. Keep refrigerated and bake conventionally, or in a microwave oven, when required.

INDEX

A

al dente, 28
alphabetti, 12
anchovies:
  Anchovy, olive, & caper
    sauce, 45
  Egg & anchovy, 44
Asian noodle salad, 40
Aubergine lasagne with
  cheese sauce, 58-9

B

bacon, 18
  Carbonara, 43
balsamic vinegar, 18
basil, 15
  colouring, 21
béchamel sauce, 41
beetroot colouring, 21
black pepper, 16
Bolognese sauce, 48, 60
buckwheat spaghetti, 9
Butter & cream sauce, 49

C

calorie count, 8
cannelloni, 12, 25
  Cannelloni with chicken
    & mozzarella, 63
capers, 18

Anchovy, olive, & caper
  sauce, 45
cappelletti, 10, 25
cappellini, 9
Carbonara, 43
cheese:
  cheese filling, 53
  Cheese tortellini with
    smoked salmon, 56-7
  cooking cheese, 52
  Gorgonzola sauce, 44
  Parmesan, 30
  Three cheese sauce, 52
  types, 19
  Chicken, cannelloni with
    mozzarella &, 63
chifferi rigati, 10
Chinese moons with
  lemon sauce, 66-7
Chinese noodles, 13
clam sauce, 50-1
Classic béchamel sauce, 41
colouring pasta, 21
conchiglie, 11
cooking pasta, 27-31
crusts, avoiding, 30
cutting pasta, 24-5

D

deep-frying, 29
defrosting pasta sauces, 69
ditalini, 11, 12
drainer, 28
draining pasta, 29
dried pasta, 8
  storage, 68
drying pasta, 23, 24

E

eggs:
  carbonara, 43
  Egg & anchovy, 44
  egg pasta, 14
  egg pasta dough, 20-3
  testing for freshness, 14

F

farfalle, 8, 10
fettuccine, 24
fibre, 8
flavourings, 21
flour, 14
folded-stuffed pasta, 25
freezing pesto, 42
freezing sauces, 69
fresh pasta, 8,
  storing, 68
Fresh pasta dough, 20-3
Fusilli al pesto, 13
  Fusilli & pesto salad,
    34-5

G

garlic, 16
garnishes, 31
gigantoni, 11
Gorgonzola, 44
grating Parmesan, 30

H

ham, 18
herbs, 15

I

ingredients, 14-19

J

juniper berries, 16

L

lasagne, 12
  Aubergine lasagne with cheese sauce, 58–9
  Lasagne bolognese, 60
long pasta, how to eat, 31

M

Macaroni with fennel & raisins, 61
marjoram, 15
meat filling, 53
millerighe, 11
Minestrone soup, 32
mushroom colouring, 21

N

noodles, 13
  Asian noodle salad, 40
  Vegetable noodle soup, 33
nutmeg, 16

O

olive oil, 14
  Olive oil & garlic dressing, 52
olives, 18
  Anchovy, olive & caper sauce, 45
onions, 16
oregano, 15
oriental pasta, 13
orzo, 12

P

pan-frying, 29
pansoti, 25
pappardelle, 9

Parmesan cheese, 19, 30
Parmigiano-Reggiano 19, 30
parsley, 15
  Hot parsley pasta salad, 36–7
pasta drainer, 28
pasta machine, 23
pesto sauce, 42
  Fusilli and pesto salad, 34–5
pine nuts, 18
piping fillings, 25
primavera sauce, 47

R

Ragù Bolognese, 48, 60
ravioli, 12, 26
  with saffron ricotta, 62
Red clam sauce, 50–1
refrigerating sauces, 69
reheating pasta, 69
ribbons, 24
rigatoni, 11
  Baked rigatoni with meatballs, 64–5
rolling pin, 22
ruoti, 11

S

saffron, 16
  colouring, 21
sage, 15
salads, 34–40
  storing, 68
sandwich-stuffed pasta, 26
sauces, 41–52
  freezing, 69
  matching to pasta, 13
Seafood sauce, 44
short pasta, 10–11
soups, 32–3

spaghetti, 9, 13
spices, 16
spinach, 18
  flavouring, 21
  Spinach & cheese pinwheels, 54–5
stellini, 12
sticking, preventing, 30
storing pasta, 68–9
strozzapreti, 11
stuffed pasta, 12, 53–67
  folded-stuffed, 25–6

T

tagliarini, 9
tagliatelle, 9
thyme, 15
tomatoes, 17
  flavouring, 21
  Fresh tomato sauce, 41
  purée, 17
  Spicy tomato & bacon sauce, 46
  Tomato & basil sauce, 45
tortellini, 25, 62
  Cheese tortellini with smoked salmon, 56–7
tortelloni verde, 12
tubetti lunghi, 10
Tuna pasta salad Niçoise, 38–9

V–W

Vegetable noodle soup, 33
vinegar, balsamic, 18
White clam sauce, 50–1

Acknowledgments

Dorling Kindersley would like to thank Hilary Bird for compiling the index, Ann Kaye for proof-reading, Murdo Culver for design assistance, Bella Pringle and Alexa Stace for editorial assistance, and Mark Bracey for computer assistance.

Photography
KEY: t *top*; b *bottom*; c *centre*; l *left*; r *right*

All photography by Amanda Heywood, David Murray, and Clive Streeter except for:
Martin Brigdale 42 all except cl; Philip Dowell 10tr, br; 11tr, br; 12tr, tl; 32tr, cr; 61tr; 62cl, c; Stephen Oliver 32br; Roger Phillips 8bl; 12c, bl, bc, br; 16br, bl, cr; 2tr; 53; Susanna Price 30br; Matthew Ward 7; 28bl; 68; 69tr; Jerry Young 25tr; 26 all except tr.

The recipe on page 62 originally appeared in *Little Library Pasta* by Jill Norman (Dorling Kindersley 1990).